D1743876

101 THINGS
YOU NEVER KNEW ABOUT
WALT DISNEY WORLD

101 THINGS

YOU NEVER KNEW ABOUT WALT DISNEY WORLD

An Unauthorized Look at Tributes, Little
Touches, and Inside Jokes

Kevin Yee

Ultimate Orlando Press
Orlando, Florida

101 Things You Never Knew About Walt Disney World: An
Unauthorized Look at Tributes, Little Touches, and Inside Jokes
by Kevin Yee

Published by
ULTIMATE ORLANDO PRESS
www.ultimateorlando.com

All rights reserved. No part of this book may be reproduced or
transmitted in any form or by any means, electronic or mechanical,
including photocopying, recording or by any information storage
and retrieval system without written permission from the author,
except for the inclusion of brief quotations in a review.

Cover design by "The Dozak"
Copyright © 2007 Ultimate Orlando Press

This book makes reference to various Disney copyrighted characters,
trademarks, marks, and registered marks owned by The Walt Disney
Company and Disney Enterprises, Inc.

101 Things You Never Knew About Walt Disney World is not
endorsed by, sponsored by, or connected with The Walt Disney
Company and/or Disney Enterprises, Inc. in any way.

ISBN-10: 0-9773758-0-3
ISBN-13: 978-0-9773758-0-6
Library of Congress Control Number: 2005910933

FIRST EDITION
Fourth Printing
Printed in the United States of America

To Michelle

No book is written alone. This one came into being with the patient help of numerous sources, readers, and friends, among them **Tony Baxter, Bruce Gordon, Joe Lanzisero, Kim Irvine, Doug Hartwell, Bob Baranick, Eddie Sotto, Bob Gurr, Chris Merritt, Josh Shipley, Bill Watkins, Jim Korkis, Duncan Dickson, Reed Cunningham, Eric Main, Doobie and Rebekah Moseley, Jeff Lange, Matt Heitzmann, Dan Morrow,** and **Jorge Morales**. My coauthor on the Disneyland books, **Jason Schultz**, was invaluable in the early research process for this book as well.

Finally, I want to give thanks to my wife **Michelle** and son **Devon** for their patience and understanding during the genesis of this book. They enrich my life every day.

Introduction

The constantly-evolving nature of Walt Disney World is part of its allure. Every year the theme parks reinvent and redefine themselves, often by introducing new attractions and replacing older ones. The designers of the attractions, called Imagineers, frequently show their reverence for "what came before" by re-using small reminders of former rides in newer ones.

These homages are scattered about like Easter Eggs left for visitors to find, and are sometimes accompanied by other tributes: inside jokes about thematic elements, re-used figures and characters, even personal touches like the designers' own initials incorporated into thematic elements in the show. These tributes and inside references deposit layers of meaning and history to a form of entertainment often enjoyed on the strengths of its surface value alone. They impart ulterior significance to the attractions and the people who design them, and ultimately remind us why we found them so special in the first place.

The level of attention paid to even the least noticeable of details helps impart to Walt Disney World its distinctive magic and keeps the parks a cut above the competition. Savoring the details will enrich the experience, no matter how often you visit.

Kevin Yee

Magic
Kingdom

1

A bench in Town Square honors Roy O. Disney, who opened Walt Disney World after his brother passed away.

Walt died before his vision for an East Coast vacation destination could be realized, but his brother Roy carried forward the plans for the Magic Kingdom. For this service, a bronze statue of Roy sitting with Minnie Mouse on a bench adorns Town Square. The form and composition of Roy's statue are deliberate echoes of the more visible "Partners" statue of Walt with Mickey, at the other end of Main Street.

FURTHERMORE: The scale of buildings and vehicles is one immediately noticeable difference between the parks. Because Disneyland was built on less acreage, everything was often built to a small scale, utilizing "forced perspective" (features get smaller than real life as they get taller) to make buildings look bigger. While the Magic Kingdom also uses forced perspective, it does so with more subtlety and less often, because the park was built on more acres and offers the ability to create vehicles and buildings at full size.

2

Photographs below the Main Street Train Station honor the Disney company's long history with trains.

Pictures adorning the walls of the stroller rental area show the Magic Kingdom's locomotives in their former industrial lives, and other nearby photographs feature Walt Disney and the miniature backyard train at his Holmby Hills estate. One information board makes casual reference to former Santa Fe company executives, whose names are also those of the locomotives at Disneyland. A second board gives subtle tribute to Disney employee and fellow train enthusiast Ward Kimball and his personal full-sized train on his property, which he dubbed Grizzly Flats. Further signs explain how Walt's love of trains contributed to the idea that became Disneyland and the Magic Kingdom.

FURTHERMORE: While Walt Disney's role in the company's theme parks is undeniable and his tributes—such as the "Partners" statue with Mickey Mouse in the center of the Magic Kingdom—are equally hard to miss, his brother Roy Disney was the one who lived to see Walt Disney World opened in 1971, and so he is honored in today's Magic Kingdom with a statue sitting on a bench in Town Square. The statue of Roy posing with Minnie Mouse offers a bookend to Main Street, with the other bookend to be found in the highly visible statue of Walt and Mickey at the end of the street.

3

The fire station on Main Street pays tribute to the year the Magic Kingdom opened.

Though above-ground construction started in 1969, the Magic Kingdom did not open until 1971. In honor of that year, the fire station purports to be "Engine Co. 71" in brass lettering visible high on the building's front side. A sign halfway up Main Street at one doorway near the Athletic Club pays tribute to the Cast Members at Walt Disney World throughout the years, and mentions that this "casting agency" has been open since '71.

FURTHERMORE: Up the road, a sign above one doorway for the Emporium claims it was established in 1901—the year Walt Disney was born. A colorful mural near the ceiling just inside this section of the Emporium also mentions 1901. Main Street purports to be a sanitized version of a typical small American town circa 1890-1910, a period during which Walt was heavily influenced by his time spent as a child in one such small town, Marceline, Missouri. Traces of this time frame are everywhere. For instance, one store features an old-style telephone near a wood-burning oven. Antique mutoscopes, which approximate a film by flipping through static pictures, entertain visitors at the Main Street train station. They were moved here when the Penny Arcade was converted to a shop, while other mutoscopes found homes at the Boardwalk resort and the prop warehouse at Disney's Hollywood Studios's Backlot Tour.

4

Many of the windows along the second story of Main Street are decorated with the names of important individuals that made significant contributions to Walt Disney World.

From General Joe Potter, the construction expert who oversaw the building of the Magic Kingdom, to Earl Vilmer, who renovated the Walt Disney World Railroad locomotives, these windows give credit to the often unsung people whose years of hard work enabled the Magic Kingdom to thrive.

FURTHERMORE: At Disneyland, where the tradition of using such second-story windows to honor important company officials began, a majority of the people honored are artists and engineers (dubbed "Imagineers") who helped build and design that park. At the Magic Kingdom, there are more managers and administrators listed, such as the onetime head of Walt Disney World security, the chief Walt Disney World accountant, or the director of the Walt Disney World paint shop.

5

Windows above the Market House on Main Street list the names of the shell companies used to buy the land Walt Disney World would be built upon.

The forty-seven square miles eventually purchased for Walt Disney World had to be bought from multiple owners who would have raised their asking price if they knew Disney was behind the acquisitions, so Walt used secrecy to hide his intentions. To make the purchases, he sent unknown emissaries that ostensibly operated for companies which turned out to not actually exist, such as Tomahawk Properties, Latin American Development, Bay Lake Properties, Reedy Creek Ranch Lands, Compass East Corporation, and Ayefour Corporation (a subtle reference to the nearby I-4 interstate freeway)

FURTHERMORE: While the buildings on Disneyland's Main Street were inspired by architecture in Marceline, Missouri and Fort Collins, Colorado (the boyhood towns of Walt Disney and Harper Goff, one of the original park designers), at Walt Disney World an effort was made to pay homage to towns on the East Coast. For instance, the tower in Philadelphia's city hall gave the Magic Kingdom's city hall its distinctive look. Similarly, the porches at the Emporium can be traced to the Grand Union Hotel in Sarasota Springs, NY—a city that provided the inspiration for several other buildings in the Magic Kingdom.

6

Walt Disney is honored on a window above the Plaza Ice Cream Parlor.

Both Roy O. Disney and his son, Roy E. Disney, have windows on Main Street that acknowledge their lasting influence on the company. At Disneyland, Walt Disney didn't want a window dedicated to himself, but when he died, park designers sought to honor him in this fashion at Walt Disney World. Walt's window is one of the few such tribute windows that face Cinderella Castle, marking the location as a place of honor. This is actually Walt's second window on Main Street; the other being the highly visible window on the railroad station, facing out toward the park's main entrance.

FURTHERMORE: A different way to conceive of the location for Walt's second window is to consider all of Main Street as the opening credits of a motion picture. If the windows on the buildings all along the street give credit to those "behind the camera" making the park come true, Walt's name appropriately comes both first and last, as he is the director of the entire production. It is no coincidence that most of the early Imagineers were artists from movie studios, familiar primarily with storytelling and movie-style showmanship. For this reason, Walt and his artists constructed visual "weenies" to lure visitors to the next "reel" of the "motion picture," such as a castle for Fantasyland or a tall white steamship for Frontierland.

7

An unused structure around the Central Plaza was once a loading dock for a boat ride.

The Plaza Swan Boats circled the Central Plaza in the Magic Kingdom's early years, gliding along tracks at an automatically-controlled pace and offering a tranquil journey around the castle and its carefully manicured lawns. More of a relaxing atmosphere ride than a mode of transportation, the Swan Boats unfortunately suffered from low capacity and eventually succumbed to the march of time. Like the dock in Liberty Square once home to flat-bottomed keelboats that freely roamed the Rivers of America, the Swan Boat dock has no current function apart from serving as a reminder of the ride once housed here.

FURTHERMORE: The loading dock today may be little more than shelter from the elements, but the tracks still exist along the bottom of the moat around the Central Plaza. The front of the Swan Boats were shaped like giant white swans—a thematic nod to Disneyland's longstanding tradition of housing real swans in the moat around its castle. The pathway to the loading dock is still marked by topiary shrubs carefully groomed in the shape of swans.

8

One portion of the audio on the Tomorrowland Transit Authority honors a former attraction called Mission to Mars.

At one point on the Tomorrowland Transit Authority, we hear terminal-style announcements paging "Mr. Morrow, Mr. Tom Morrow"—a reference to the animatronic "host" of Mission to Mars, also wittily named Tom Morrow. Mission to Mars was replaced by Alien Encounter, which in turn gave way to Stitch's Great Escape. The Mr. Morrow animatronic was at one time instead referred to as "Mr. Johnson," and it's no accident we also hear Mr. Johnson paged on the Tomorrowland Transit Authority.

FURTHERMORE: The general layout of Stitch's Great Escape, and Alien Encounter before it, can be traced directly to Mission to Mars. In the original attraction, the preshow featured an interactive conversation with Mr. Morrow as he stood in the control room. Then, visitors moved to one of two circular theaters set up to see viewscreens in the floor, ceiling, and sides of the theater, which captured the action as our rocket ship blasted off, made its way to Mars, and returned home. Today's attraction adds hardware, particularly in the center of the theater and in the interactive seat restraints, but the layout of rooms, its design, and even some of the viewscreens remain largely the same.

9

The model visible from the Tomorrowland Transit Authority ride was created as the original vision of EPCOT.

The first idea for EPCOT (which stood for Experimental Prototype Community of Tomorrow) was a revolutionary new kind of city planned to be built on Disney property. The model for it, now named Progress City, was created to show off Walt's concept. While this vision of EPCOT never materialized, part of the enormous model lives on in Tomorrowland.

FURTHERMORE: The dreams of a community of tomorrow do exist, in a fashion, in today's Tomorrowland. The land is themed to represent an alien spaceport, with robots, aliens, and humans commingling in one peaceful society. The show narration from the Tomorrowland Transit Authority furthers this idea by mentioning a League of Planets headquartered here, as well as references to elements typical of a community, such as the Interplanetary Convention Center and Chamber of Commerce. While the Tomorrowland at Disneyland Paris draws inspiration from Jules Verne, the Magic Kingdom's vision of the future is derived from Buck Rogers and Flash Gordon, with cheesy flying saucers serving as decorations throughout the land.

10

An extra vehicle from the Astro-Orbitor alongside the Tomorrowland Transit Authority was placed here because of a former Tomorrowland attraction.

The Astro-Orbitor vehicle is seen with an alien aboard, prepared to launch into space, just after the Progress City model. This reference to Tomorrowland's status as a spaceport for aliens dates to the mid-1990s, when an attraction called Alien Encounter replaced Mission to Mars. On the occasion of its addition, the entire land was given a facelift and re-conceived as a spaceport. Without Alien Encounter, Tomorrowland today might still be a disjointed celebration of futurism and space travel without a sense of a specific place like a spaceport.

FURTHERMORE: Murals in the Merchant of Venus store call further attention to the alien spaceport concept. Designed to show off the rest of Tomorrowland as if the walls were transparent windows rather than a painting, these murals behind the cash registers show the familiar Tomorrowland architecture and depict aliens of all types, in the same style and with the same cartoon sensibilities as Stitch, wandering about as the sole inhabitants of the land.

11

A set piece in Buzz Lightyear's Space Ranger Spin is left unaltered from the previous attraction in this location.

The rotating red light amid fog just prior to the theater-like finale of Buzz Lightyear is actually a remnant from the previous inhabitant, Dreamflight, which was also known as Take Flight for many years. This set was originally meant to signify our vehicles entering a giant turbine engine (the ride was first sponsored by Eastern Airlines, then Delta Airlines), and the red frame overhead as we enter the area still remains, though it is now labeled an escape hatch. One other feature remained from the old track layout: the "speed tunnel" near the end of the attraction was left intact, but given a new film so riders could blast the projection of Zurg's spaceship.

FURTHERMORE: The Buzz Lightyear attraction uses the same drive mechanism and even the entire track layout unaltered from Take Flight—itself an update of the original attraction here, If You Had Wings. Visitors on the Tomorrowland Transit Authority (TTA) now peer into one room of Buzz Lightyear's Space Ranger Spin, but when Dreamflight occupied this space, they could glance down on both sides of the TTA track and see into separate rooms. These days, unused windows on the left side of the TTA track give testament to the location where visitors used to sneak a peak at the second room.

12

Wooden cutouts of chickens in Buzz Lightyear's Space Ranger Spin also come from the attraction which preceded it.

Three chickens just in front of our vehicle in the volcano room of Buzz Lightyear had once occupied the first room of Dreamflight, where whimsical cutout figures celebrated the rural nature of early flight. Another show feature retained from Dreamflight can be seen in the first few scenes, where cloud-shaped bumps alongside the vehicle track frame what visitors can see near the floor. Now painted black, these billowy humps originally represented clouds, in keeping with the aeronautical theme of Dreamflight.

FURTHERMORE: The cylindrical batteries seen throughout the attraction contain their own inside joke: they are "Made in Glendale," a reference to the home of Walt Disney Imagineering in Glendale, California. Additional versions of these batteries can also be seen in the attraction's queue and exit area.

13

Hidden jokes in the Space Mountain queue reveal designers' sense of humor.

At the very beginning of the indoor queue is a large departure board displaying supposed flights around the galaxy. Among the real stars mentioned are puns and verbal gags. For instance, Sirius is followed by the star 'Real Sirius'. Others simply must be read out loud to be fully appreciated, such as 'World Ceres', 'Gamma Gammpa', 'Mensa Quadrant', and 'Beta Beleevit'.

FURTHERMORE: The Great Movie Ride also folds in numerous witticisms in the small print not often read closely. This is most noticeable in the spaceship Nostromo, the section dedicated to the movie *Alien*, where a monitor off to the side uses very small typeface to list names of people involved with the movie as well as tongue-in-cheek references to Walt Disney World itself.

14

The term "FX-1" seen in various places at Space Mountain is a remnant of the attraction's former sponsor.

The illuminated star chart at the beginning of the queue bears the words FX-1, as does the giant ship seen above the final upramp at the start of the ride. This same phrase is also visible on the nearby control booth. All refer to shipping giant FedEx, who as sponsor was also responsible for installing the exit sequences set up like an intergalactic matter transporter beaming boxes around the galaxy.

FURTHERMORE: Space Mountain was built in the 1970s as the world's first enclosed roller-coaster to operate in the dark, and originally sponsored by music company RCA. The opening date of January, 1975 is commemorated on the backs of the spacesuits worn by the upside-down astronauts seen when on the first upramp of the ride. When FedEx took over as sponsor of the ride in 1990s, they created the dioramas still visible today at the exit to the ride, including a mechanical dog crafted as a subtle reference to RCA's mascot Nipper, complete with his trademark cocked head and floppy ears.

15

The vacant building in Tomorrowland with a waterfall was once the Skyway station.

Until 1999, a Skyway attraction allowed for one-way rides between Fantasyland and Tomorrowland. The building near Space Mountain had been both the Tomorrowland anchor for the ride as well as the overnight storage facility for the buckets. The Skyway is still referenced on a brass plaque near the center of Tomorrowland that provides a schematic map of the land.

FURTHERMORE: The Swiss chalet in Fantasyland is the other of the two Skyway stations at the Magic Kingdom, and this building also remains in its original location atop a hill at the extreme western edge of Fantasyland. Near to the station in today's Fantasyland, one patch of roughly circular ground with a different texture from the rest of the walkway gives testament to an area that once held a support pylon for the ride, and was filled in after the pylon was removed.

16

Colorful tents in Mickey's Toontown Fair date back to this land's original theme.

In 1988, when Mickey Mouse turned 60, the company staged a world-wide celebration, and a temporary land then known as Mickey's Birthdayland sprang up behind Tomorrowland. It utilized temporary-looking façades and giant striped tents to represent the various houses of the Disney characters. The success of Mickey's Birthdayland caused it to be held over as Mickey's Starland, and gave rise to the idea of Mickey's Toontown in Anaheim, a theme more in keeping with the movie *Who Framed Roger Rabbit*. Because Mickey and friends "lived" in Toontown in Anaheim, the permanent Orlando structures that replaced Mickey's Starland, and yet kept the striped tents, were renamed Mickey's Toontown Fair.

FURTHERMORE: A barn once used to house live animals in an area called Grandma Duck's Farm was kept as a show piece for Goofy's Barnstormer. Now called only "the Barnstormer," references to Goofy abound, including the Goofy scarecrow, Goofy's pants used as a windsock, Goofy's outline on the barn as if he had crashed through it, and more subtle references like the "G" on the tail of the last car of the coaster and the pump containing "Goofoline" in the loading zone.

17

The statue of Cornelius Coot in Mickey's Toontown Fair testifies to the dual nature of the area's original theme.

When Mickey's Birthdayland opened in 1988, signs throughout the area made reference to the town as Duckburg. Although *Who Framed Roger Rabbit* (1988) would eventually provide the theme in the form of Toontown, the popularity of *DuckTales* (1987) on TV argued for Duckburg as the more recognizable name. Few of the decorations or buildings from this early land have survived the transition to Mickey's Toontown Fair, but the statue of Cornelius Coot, the founder of Duckburg, remains in today's land.

FURTHERMORE: Officially, there is only one Toontown, and it's located behind Fantasyland in Anaheim's Disneyland. To keep this mythology alive, designers chose to make Orlando's version a fair rather than Toontown itself. That the characters have houses on both coasts isn't really addressed, nor is the dichotomy in the form of a fair that also somehow includes residences for Mickey and Minnie. In this respect, the land continues the tradition of schizophrenic theming: just as Mickey's Birthdayland was Duckburg (never mind that Mickey supposedly lived in Mouseville), the land today is both a fair and a housing development.

18

A painting in the Many Adventures of Winnie the Pooh honors the former occupant of this space, Mr. Toad's Wild Ride.

The left wall of Owl's house features paintings, one of which shows Mr. Toad handing a piece of paper marked "DEED" over to Owl, implying a transfer of this property from Toad to Winnie the Pooh and his pals. A second painting on the opposite side of the room has "fallen" onto the floor showing Moley, another character from Mr. Toad's Wild Ride, standing with Winnie the Pooh. A third painting, back on the left side of the vehicle in the same room, shows Owl smiling through a handlebar moustache in a tribute to Winky, yet another character from the Toad movie and attraction. To top it off, in this picture Owl is wearing a skimmer straw hat, just like Toad was at the end of his movie.

FURTHERMORE: Just outside the exit to the Haunted Mansion, a graveyard ostensibly for pets includes statues and grave markers for dogs, cats, and birds. Back in the far corner, a humble statue of Mr. Toad himself provides a whimsical tribute to this character, who is "dead" because his ride can no longer be found at the Magic Kingdom. His tombstone reads: "Here Lies Toad / Sad But True / Much Less Profitable / Than Pooh"

19

Coats of arms in Cinderella's Royal Table honor people important to the Disney organization.

Coats of arms scattered throughout the interior of the castle, especially the waiting area and the main dining room of the restaurant, refer to the family names of many individuals who helped design and make the Disney theme parks a reality. Some of these symbols are also visible on the stained glass windows and can be seen from the outside of the castle, in the courtyard that is home to the carrousel.

FURTHERMORE: A large space was set aside in the upper areas of the castle when it was first built to serve as an apartment for the Disney family, but it was never fully built or decorated until the 2007 promotion "Year of a Million Dreams." Finally outfitted with furniture and lavish trappings, the apartment remains off-limits for normal public viewing, apart from contest winners. Visitors on the outside can catch a glimpse, though, by looking at the castle from the back side and spying three stained-glass windows 2/3rds of the way up the castle, off to one side.

20

Pooh's Playful Spot pays tribute to the ride which preceded it on this location.

Visitors who step inside the room carved out of the base of Pooh's tree will notice a sleek blue shape above the doorway, visible only from the inside. This is meant to represent a submarine, for the area was once home to a fleet of half-submerged subs that traveled through a lagoon in an attraction called 20,000 Leagues Under the Sea, loosely based on Disney's 1954 movie of the same name.

FURTHERMORE: Fantasyland is the area of Walt Disney World that most directly pays tribute to Disney movies, but not all homages are obvious at first glance. A visual trick at a fountain behind Cinderella Castle thematizes that movie by using staging alone. Formally known as La Fontaine de Cendrillon (Cinderella's Fountain), and informally called the "rags to riches" fountain, this statue of Cinderella shows her wearing her housecleaning outfit (the "rags"), but when viewed from a low elevation, such as the height of a child, the decorations on the wall behind her head resolve into a crown that appears to sit perfectly atop her hair (the "riches"). Designed to be visible to children rather than adults, this visual trick captures the main action of the movie without needing any moving parts.

21

Mickey Mouse's role as conductor in Philharmagic harkens back to a previous attraction at this very location.

Before Mickey's Philharmagic opened in 2003, this space was occupied by a live-action puppet show called Legend of the Lion King. Before that, it was the Fantasyland Theater, and this space until 1980 was home to the Mickey Mouse Revue, a musical show performed by minimalist animatronics of Disney characters, singing songs led by none other than bandleader Mickey Mouse. Walt Disney had made mention of plans for an animatronic show of all the Disney characters before his death, and this show was moved in its entirety to Tokyo Disneyland, where it still plays today.

FURTHERMORE: The figures of the seven dwarves were duplicated for the 1994 refurbishment of Snow White's Scary Adventures. Surprisingly, this was not the only instance of recycling the figures from this show. The Alice character, the Mad Hatter, the March Hare, and some flower heads were also removed and taken to Disneyland in 1984, for the major refurbishment of Fantasyland on the West Coast.

22

One doll in "it's a small world" pays tribute to an artist partly responsible for the ride's look and feel.

Joyce Carlson, an Imagineer who assisted in creating the original ride when it premiered at the 1964 World's Fair and later Disneyland, is represented as a doll underneath the Eiffel Tower early in the attraction. Joyce was later placed in charge of installing and maintaining the other versions of the ride around the globe, including the Orlando one. Like Joyce herself, her doll sports big black glasses.

FURTHERMORE: The tradition of using a doll to honor the architects of this attraction began at Disneyland, where a doll meant to represent Mary Blair, the primary designer on Small World and an artist whose distinctive look also graces the murals near the Monorail stop at the Contemporary Resort, can be seen halfway up the Eiffel Tower in California's version of the ride. This doll sports the same yellow coat and black pants which were Mary's trademarks. Even beyond this attraction, there is a long tradition of homages to Disney artists in the finished rides. Longtime Disney artist Herb Ryman, who created many conceptual paintings of Disney theme parks and their attractions, is honored in the second scene of Carousel of Progress by virtue of a billboard in the cityscape seen through the window, which proclaims "Herb Ryman – Attorney at Law."

23

The bronzed decorations atop the spires of "it's a small world" are exact copies of Imagineer Leota Thomas' jewelry.

When the Disneyland version of the attraction was being prepared, the sometimes fantastical earrings, pendants, and charms of its chief designer provided a sudden inspiration for the tops of the spires visible on the outdoor façade for the Anaheim attraction. The designs of her jewelry were simply copied and produced on a much larger scale for the attraction's façade. In the Orlando version of the attraction, these bronze toppings look especially like the stud earrings that inspired them, possibly because visitors exit the ride by walking through the spires and thus approach the decorations much more closely than in Anaheim.

FURTHERMORE: The exterior of the attraction is adorned with pikes, jousting lances, and shields. These decorations reinforce the theme of the area behind the castle as a medieval courtyard, with colorful tents throughout the land as if set up for a tournament.

24

Tombstones alongside the queue for the Haunted Mansion honor the Imagineers who helped build the ride.

The designers given a tribute here include Xavier Atencio (who wrote the lyrics and script for the show), Marc Davis (who was one of the main creative forces), Yale Gracey (who created many of the illusions), Wathel Rogers (who crafted many of the mechanical effects), Claude Coates (who designed the track layout), Cliff Huet (who was an interior designer), Gordon Williams (who worked with the *Audio-Animatronics*), Leota Toombs (who performed as the séance madam), Bob Sewell and Dave Burkhart (who crafted many of the models), and Chuck Myall, Fred Joerger, and Bill Martin (who were art directors on the attraction).

FURTHERMORE: The Leota tombstone just outside the entrance to the Mansion was the brainchild of Jason Surrell, an Imagineer so enamored with the Haunted Mansion that he wrote a book about the attraction, its history, and its transformation into a live-action motion picture. Every few seconds, the eyes of the face on this tombstone flutter open, look about, then close again.

25

A raven is often present when the "Ghost Host" narrator speaks in the Haunted Mansion.

Almost every time Guests hear the voice of the Ghost Host, the raven is nearby. In the original plans for the attraction, the bird was supposed to *be* the Ghost Host, the narrator of the ride. The raven, long associated with death in several cultures, is present in the conservatory on the moving coffin, in the séance room on the chair, in the Ballroom along the rear wall, right outside the attic, and at the end of the graveyard, just as visitors enter the crypt.

FURTHERMORE: One of the Mansion's creepiest optical effects, the busts in the library that appear to turn their heads in sync as the "Doom Buggies" pass by them, actually owes its existence to Great Moments with Mr. Lincoln, a Disneyland-only forerunner to the Hall of Presidents. Designers happened to pass by a negative mold of the Lincoln head—an inverted cast from which the actual head would be made—when they realized that its inverted nature always resulted in the unnerving effect.

26

Disembodied arms holding torches at the exit to Haunted Mansion are but one of many remnants of a "Museum of the Weird" concept.

There was a Walt-era idea to create a museum in Disneyland's New Orleans Square dedicated to strange, supernatural, and occult items, such as might be found in a gypsy's wagon. These concepts were incorporated into the Haunted Mansion in the form of furniture and trappings of the house that seem to be alive but disembodied or unnatural.

FURTHERMORE: Besides the arms holding torches, other examples include the clock striking 13 (watch for a face with fangs, and the clock's pendulum as a tail) or the gypsy-like cart outside Orlando's Haunted Mansion selling merchandise. These designs were all the work of one Imagineer named Rolly Crump.

27

The ghostly woman in a rocking chair at the Ballroom scene of the Haunted Mansion is a duplicate figure from another attraction.

The *Audio-Animatronics* figure is a duplicate of the grandmother in Carousel of Progress. The first versions of the two rides were conceived and built in the 1960s, so it made sense to re-use the molds of existing *Audio-Animatronics* whenever possible.

FURTHERMORE: The Haunted Mansion adds ambiance in dozens of ways, many of them subtle touches that don't call attention to themselves. For instance, horseshoe prints in the cement out front are meant to imply that the phantom horse pulling the black hearse might not be simply ethereal after all. Up in the second-story windows, a shadowy figure is sometimes seen moving around with a lantern.

28

The Haunted Mansion is modeled after houses from the Hudson River Valley.

Houses built in the 18th century in the picturesque Hudson River Valley, now a National Heritage area and home to well-preserved dwellings from several different epochs in American history, provided the thematic inspiration for the general look to the Haunted Mansion. The Hudson River Valley is also the setting for the legend of Sleepy Hollow and the Headless Horseman—a perfect thematic fit for the Haunted Mansion. At the other end of Liberty Square, an eatery named "Sleepy Hollow Refreshments" provides a thematic bookend for the land.

FURTHERMORE: References to colonial history are visible throughout the land. On the bridge from the Central Plaza, crates marked "tea" make reference to the Boston Tea Party. Paul Revere's two lanterns are visible in one window facing the river near the Haunted Mansion. The Liberty Bell duplicate is the only one ever created from the same mold as the famous bell. Nearby, the Liberty Tree contains 13 lanterns to represent the 13 original colonies. Finally, the numbers "1787" atop the entrance for the Hall of Presidents is a reference to the year the U.S. Constitution was signed.

29

The *Liberty Belle* steamboat was originally named the *Richard F. Irvine.*

At first there were two steamboats plying the waters of the Rivers of America: the *Admiral Joe Fowler* and the *Richard F. Irvine*, named after two company executives who had done much to help build Walt Disney World. A dry-dock accident permanently crippled the *Fowler* when it was dropped by a crane, and after it was sidelined, the *Irvine* was renamed to the *Liberty Belle*. To honor the *Irvine*, one of its preservers was kept with the original name for several years.

FURTHERMORE: To continue the tradition of honoring these men who did so much to help the Disney company, two of the ferries used to transport guests from the Ticket and Transportation Center to the theme park, named *Magic Kingdom-1* and *Magic Kingdom-2*, were renamed to the *Admiral Joe Fowler* and *Richard F. Irvine*. A third ferry is named the *General Joe Potter*, another figure responsible for building Walt Disney World.

30

Ye Olde Christmas Shoppe is themed to represent three different stores combined over time.

Differences in furniture colors and styles, as well as highly varied wallpaper styles, point to the implied history of the merchandise location as one that conglomerated out of three different shops. Trinkets atop shelves in each area attest to the previous residents in each shop: a musician, a woodcarver, and a German family identified as Kepple (a subtle nod to Walt's grandfather, Kepple Disney). This store is not the only location to attempt to theme various rooms differently. Pinocchio Village Haus has seven rooms, each highlighting a different character from the movie: Geppetto, Figaro, Cleo, the Blue Fairy, Jiminy Cricket, Stromboli, and Monstro.

FURTHERMORE: The presence of three separate areas in the Christmas Shoppe can be traced to the fact that originally, there were three distinct stores here! The Christmas Shoppe replaced three separate locations: Mlle. Lafayette's Parfumerie, the Silversmith, and Old World Antiques.

31

Liberty Square and Frontierland together represent the continental United States.

While Liberty Square represents the colonies and thus the eastern seaboard, Frontierland evokes first the forested frontiers of civilization that gradually fade into the mining desert towns of the far west. Traveling from Liberty Square to the end of Frontierland is like moving across the U.S. from east to west. Splash Mountain, the most recent addition to the area, is an exception to this thematic continuity. When it was added in the early 1990s, Splash Mountain disrupted the otherwise continuous flow of "east to west", since Splash Mountain is set in the South.

FURTHERMORE: The Diamond Horseshoe is styled to represent St. Louis, so that the nearby bridge implies crossing the Mississippi into the West. The strip of colored pavement that winds through most of Liberty Square and Frontierland represents a sewage ditch, a common feature of early American towns. A similar use of pavement coloration at Epcot between the France and Morocco pavilions signifies the Straits of Gibraltar, where Europe and Africa meet.

32

Fort Langhorn on Tom Sawyer Island is a creative descendant of Walt's childhood fort.

While watching Walt dictate a revised placement for Fort Wilderness at Disneyland's Tom Sawyer Island, his brother Roy realized that Walt was re-creating a makeshift fort they had often built on a sand spit out on a river as children. Orlando's version, Fort Langhorn, was named after the author Mark Twain, whose real name was Samuel Langhorn Clemens. This fort, once called simply Fort Sam Clemens, can be seen as another recreation of Walt's childhood fort.

FURTHERMORE: Harper's Mill, a structure on Tom Sawyer Island named for Imagineer and Studio artist Harper Goff, is home to a unique Disney film reference in the form of a bluebird nest. This is an homage to the Disney cartoon *The Old Mill* (1937), primarily famous today for its introduction of the multiplane camera.

33

The staging of animal encounters on Big Thunder Mountain Railroad pays tribute to the ride which was its creative ancestor.

When Big Thunder Mountain Railroad first premiered at Disneyland, it replaced Mine Train thru Nature's Wonderland, a slow-moving train ride through desert scenes and tableaus of robotic animals interacting with their surroundings in various ways. Some of those interactions are recreated at the Magic Kingdom's version of Big Thunder Mountain Railroad, such as the bobcat taking refuge from three attacking boars atop a cactus or a face-off between a roadrunner and a snake, both of which take place in the town of Tumbleweed, and are best viewed from the passing Walt Disney World railroad.

FURTHERMORE: Two of the pigs lounging at the southern end of Tumbleweed are duplicates of the hogs squealing with joy in the mud at the end of Pirates of the Caribbean. The third (and largest) pig was transplanted here from Epcot's World of Motion pavilion after it was replaced by Test Track; that pig had been in the gondola of a hot-air balloon.

34

One gopher deep inside Splash Mountain roots for a real-life sports team.

A series of gophers pop out of gopher holes in the ground in the area just prior to the big lift hill and before the big drop. The final gopher drops down from a hole in the ceiling and loudly exclaims "FSU!" This startlingly clear reference to Florida State University comes from the Imagineer responsible for the gophers, who had graduated from FSU and remained a fan of its football team.

FURTHERMORE: Disneyland's Splash Mountain was built to utilize a motley collection of animals from the musical show America Sings. Numerous weasels in that show were deployed at Splash Mountain popping up out of gopher holes, implying the same robotic performers were now to be considered gophers! When the Orlando version was built, gophers were newly created.

35

The building housing Pirates of the Caribbean is modeled after a Cuban fortress from the 17th century.

The Castillo del Morro was built in the early 1600s to protect Havana from pirates who terrorized the area, and was considered impregnable until the Seven Years War 150 years later. The Treaty of Paris (1763) that ended the war returned Cuba to Spain, but saw Florida transfer from Spanish to British control, setting the stage for eventual American ownership. A sign just inside the entrance to the attraction honors its architectural inspiration. The Magic Kingdom originally opened without a Pirates of the Caribbean ride—designers felt that Florida's proximity to real pirate history would make the subject less well received than it had been in California, where pirates were more exotic. When crowds demanded a Pirates ride, a shorter version of Disneyland's attraction was conceived, and the Castillo del Morro fort was chosen as a model because it had meaning both to pirate history and to Florida.

FURTHERMORE: The chess board sitting between two skeletons in the queue was originally laid out with the chess pieces locked in a stalemate, with the joke being that the players sat for so long seeking a way out, they died on the spot and became skeletons.

36

Vestiges of its old sponsor remain at the Sunshine Tree Terrace.

In its early years, the Tiki Room, then known as the Tropical Serenade, was sponsored by the Florida Citrus Growers, a local association that wanted to promulgate the vision of the state as sunny, warm, and welcoming, and of course to market Florida oranges as superior to all others. It was a natural fit that the association also sponsor the nearby Sunshine Tree Terrace, which served citrus drinks. The association's mascot, the Orange Bird, even maintained a presence at the Magic Kingdom, appearing as both a walkaround character and a figurine in the artificial tree that sprouted out of the counter-service location and gave it its name.

FURTHERMORE: Although the artificial tree is long gone and the Sunshine Tree Terrace now sports a misleading name, there are reminders of the association's presence in the décor. Just under the thatched roof is a pattern repeated around the entire structure: a round, orange-colored object, clearly a reference to the citrus fruit which the association wanted to ingrain in people's minds. These painted oranges survived the transition from a sponsor-driven location to a less specific theme.

37

Addresses on the Jungle Cruise FASTPASS machines refer to other Disney destinations around the world.

The ticket-distributing machines are themed like travel trunks addressed to exotic names and locales, which were chosen because they relate to the Magic Kingdom's Jungle Cruise in scope or theme. For instance, one trunk makes reference to Trader Sam, the headhunter at the end of the Jungle Cruise in California, while another is addressed to the President of the Adventurer's Club at Pleasure Island.

FURTHERMORE: It is no coincidence that Disney's Animal Kingdom shares traits and sensibilities with the Adventurer's Club. One of designer Joe Rohde's first projects for Disney was the Adventurer's Club, which presaged his later work at Disney's Animal Kingdom on a number of levels: a mishmash of world cultures, a clutter of artifacts, and a counter-culture vibe in the entire operation. Joe was assisted in designing the Adventurer's Club by magician Doug Henning, who crafted the illusions in the show.

38

Crates near to the Swiss Family Robinson Treehouse honor people associated with the book and movie.

A crate located at the exit to the Jungle Cruise is addressed to Johann David Wyss, who authored the original novel, and it is being sent to McGuire Blvd, the joke being that Dorothy McGuire was the actress who played the mother in the movie. There is also a reference to John Mills, the actor who played Father Robinson.

FURTHERMORE: The reference to John Mills includes an address on "Bora Danno," a convoluted tribute to the actor who played son Fritz Robinson, James MacArthur. To understand the tribute, one must first know that MacArthur later portrayed Detective Danny Williams in "Hawaii Five-0," the character whose nickname was "Danno."

39

Bwana Bob's was named after comedian Bob Hope, a central figure in Disney theme park history.

This store in Adventureland, originally called the "Adventureland Kiosk," was renamed Bwana Bob's in 1985 to honor Bob Hope, who was a personal friend of Walt Disney and who had taken part in Walt Disney World's official opening years before. Bob had starred in a 1963 film named *Call Me Bwana*, which inspired the first half of the store's name. Bob was present at the opening ceremonies for several Disney parks, including Disneyland, the Magic Kingdom, and Disney's Hollywood Studios, where he officially opened the park by cutting the ceremonial opening day ribbon.

FURTHERMORE: Bob is heavily involved in one version of the story of Soviet Premier Nikita Khrushchev's desired visit to Disneyland. Celebrities at an event claimed Bob paid Disneyland a compliment in conversation with the premier's wife, prompting the premier to try to arrange a visit. When the Secret Service nixed the idea, saying they couldn't guarantee his safety, Khrushchev's visible anger was televised around the world and became an international incident. Never one to pass up an opportunity—even one he had had an inadvertent hand in creating—Bob Hope turned it into a joke during a performance in Alaska, which he called "halfway between Khrushchev and Disneyland."

Epcot

40

Numerous *Audio-Animatronics* figures in Spaceship Earth are duplicates of U.S. Presidents used elsewhere at Walt Disney World.

Because Spaceship Earth called for so many *Audio-Animatronics* figures, it was deemed simpler to make use of the molds in place for the numerous figures created for the Magic Kingdom's Hall of Presidents. Teddy Roosevelt is used twice (as an Egyptian priest and a Roman senator) but most cameos are single: Franklin Pierce and John Tyler are Islamic scholars, James Buchanan portrays Gutenberg, Dwight Eisenhower plays the lute, and Ulysses S. Grant appears as a sculptor.

FURTHERMORE: Several figures in Spaceship Earth also come from the American Adventure, which needed characters that had specific features and thus had to have its robotic creations custom-made. In Spaceship Earth, the characters are either unknowns or unfamiliar faces, and faces "borrowed" from historical figures were perfectly acceptable. Look for Andrew Carnegie at the printing press and Matthew Brady as the telegraph operator, among others.

41

Several elements in Spaceship Earth make use of authentic details to enhance the realism of the presentation.

Disney Imagineers strove to instill realism in the scenes by using authentic source material whenever possible. Therefore, the hieroglyphics on the walls in Egypt are recreations of real ones, as is the decree dictated by the nearby pharaoh. The Greek play being performed is *Oedipus Rex* by Sophocles. Even some graffiti discovered in the Roman ruins was reproduced for the set where Rome burns. The Morse code heard at the telegraph office is an announcement that the golden spike to unite the transcontinental railroad has finally been driven into the ground—lending extra symbolism to the railroad tracks which are visible outside the window behind the telegraph office.

FURTHERMORE: The vignettes in this attraction revolve around communication, especially written communication. The storyline, developed with the aid of science-fiction writer Ray Bradbury, traces a continuing metaphor of writing on walls that eventually graduates into portable, and then digital, communications.

42

One line of the narrator's monologue in Ellen's Energy Adventure pays tribute to the attraction which preceded it.

As our theater vehicles pull into the last room to hear the Final Jeopardy answers, the disembodied Jeopardy narrator waxes poetic about energy: "Energy: you make the world go around!" This line is a direct quote of the title of a song written by Robert Moline in use at the original Universe of Energy pavilion, which featured a celebrity-free variation of the same ride, sets, and movie screens, which even then combined to explain the world of energy sources, but without today's humorous narrative storyline.

FURTHERMORE: In one film, Ellen and Bill visit a solar electric plant, where Ellen discovers she can control the weather by snapping her fingers. While this footage is new, the overhead shots of the rows of mirrors at this real facility in the Mojave Desert in California date back to the film used in the original Energy attraction. This portion of the ride was named the Energy Information Center, during which a wide-format film explained the varieties and possibilities of alternative fuels.

43

Odors are projected in the swamp scene of Ellen's Energy Adventure.

To accentuate the realism of the scene, designers project faux swamp smells at the audience when the dinosaur scene begins. A similar trick was utilized in the former Horizons attraction, and is still used at Soarin'. Pleasant smells are even pumped out onto Main Street in the Magic Kingdom from the Main Street Bakery, the better to improve the mood of pedestrians (and just possibly convince them to buy some candy). The pumping of fake odors is accomplished through the use of a machine dubbed a smellitzer, a reference to guns named howitzers in use during World War II that fired large shells. A smellitzer, of course, is considerably smaller, and was created by longtime Imagineer John Hench.

FURTHERMORE: The widescreen animation of earth's formation seen in Ellen's Energy Adventure is a holdover from the original attraction, and historically significant for its use of a multiplane camera to create the illusion of traveling through an animated three dimensional world. Originally invented in the 1930s, the multiplane camera had sat unused at the Disney Studios for over twenty years when it was resurrected for the Energy pavilion. This original multiplane camera is now on display at the One Man's Dream exhibit in Disney's Hollywood Studios.

44

Mission: Space honors its predecessor by displaying the old logo in the gift shop.

Housed in a diamond-shaped building where Mission: Space now stands, Horizons offered a ride through sets and movie screens that celebrated futurism, using an "Omnimover" ride system like the one still in use at the Haunted Mansion. The logo for Horizons, a stylized set of straight lines through a central circle, can be seen on the front side of the counter in the gift shop at the attraction's exit. That same logo from Horizons can also be found in today's queue at the center of the gravity wheel, which was a giant set piece from the movie *Mission to Mars* that had to be modified to fit into this building.

FURTHERMORE: While Horizons celebrated our accumulated visions of the future, including ones that never happened, Mission: Space maintains a more realistic veneer. The lunar rover hanging from the ceiling in the queue, for instance, is a real specimen on loan from the Smithsonian museum, and is one of the few rovers built by NASA that is not currently on the moon.

45

A video playing in one monitor at the mission control room of Mission: Space's queue honors the attraction's creative ancestor.

The illuminated but deserted mission control room seen at the end of the queue is a tribute all by itself to a similar set from Mission to Mars, the theme park attraction once found at Disneyland at the Magic Kingdom. The homage is made much more explicit by a brief movie clip on one of the console monitors that shows an albatross coming in for a "crash landing." This exact video figured prominently as comic relief in the Mission to Mars control room preshow, but at Mission: Space it only shows every once in a while, as it is part of a much longer loop of other videos.

FURTHERMORE: Our journey on Mission: Space takes place at the fictional International Space Training Center (ISTC), ostensibly in the year 2036. In an attempt to make the fantasy as realistic as possible, designers created as many details as they could which were based on space travel facts, not inventions. Therefore, quotes by famous people associated with the space industry dot the entrance area, and the nearby model of the moon is decorated with the 29 locations where vehicles from earth landed on the moon. The one area highlighted in red marks the location of mankind's first steps on the moon.

46

A car in the Test Track queue area honors the attraction which preceded it.

The white car elevated on blocks, seen near the start of the queue for Test Track, was used in the previous pavilion to stand on this spot, the World of Motion. That attraction celebrated the evolution of mankind's ability to travel on the ground, and in particular the role played by the automobile. While the car was displayed as a normal-looking street model in World of Motion, for Test Track's queue it has been stripped down just to its skeleton.

FURTHERMORE: The sponsor for the transportation pavilion, first as World of Motion and then Test Track, has been General Motors from the beginning. The exit to the attraction has always had a showroom for GM cars and prototypes, though the "Transcenter" theme to the World of Motion's exit area included more diverse offerings, such as the brief animated film "Water Engine" or the vaudeville robot performers "Bird and the Robot."

47

Signs in the queue and ride at Test Track allude to the attraction's planned opening date.

A green highway sign reading "Florida 97" at the end of the queue in Test Track (and seen again at the split between Track-A and Track-B in the middle of the attraction) was meant to refer to the attraction's opening date, but the reference is garbled because the ride opened two years behind schedule. Originally scheduled to open in May 1997, the attraction had all of its show elements (including these tribute signs) installed on time, but its experimental ride mechanisms led to delays and the ride was not ready for the public until March 1999.

FURTHERMORE: The driver of the semi-truck that almost hits our car in Test Track is a former president. A dark alley between the winding S-turns of the hills and the crash test is punctuated by the sudden appearance of a semi-truck, which forces our vehicle to swerve. Because the event is so brief and so sudden, and because the truck shines its headlines directly at the car, few visitors notice who is driving: a cardboard cutout of former president Lyndon Baines Johnson. He is rendered even more unrecognizable with accoutrements such as a hat and sunglasses.

48

The lifeguard station visible early in the queue for The Seas With Nemo and Friends includes a tribute to the original Living Seas pavilion.

The original pavilion cultivated the fiction that visitors were taken deep below the surface to an undersea research facility named Seabase Alpha. The lifeguard stand prominently displays the number 5A, a veiled reference to the initials for Seabase Alpha (using a numeral instead of a letter).

FURTHERMORE: Those seeking hidden characters will note the Hidden Nemo and Hidden Squirt in the cut glass at the end of the loading dock. Others seeking yet more references to the former pavilion must wait for the end of the ride. Mr. Ray's overhead voice at the unload dock exclaims "Sea Cab knowledge, that's why we explore!"—a reference to the original "sea cab" vehicles that traversed the fish tank, without additional theming.

49

A casual reference in the sea cab voiceover honors a longtime Disney voice actor.

In the voiceover, we hear mention of Commander Fulton, a reference to voice actor Fulton Burley, the voice of Michael in the Tiki Room. He worked a total of 25 years at Disneyland's Golden Horseshoe Revue, alongside Wally Boag (also present in the Tiki Room as José). In the Magic Kingdom's "Under New Management" show, the role of Fritz is still played by Thurl Ravenscroft, though Pierre is now played by Jerry Orbach, better known as the voice of Lumiere from *Beauty and the Beast*.

FURTHERMORE: Fulton Burley enjoys numerous tributes at Walt Disney World. In addition to the reference at the Seas with Nemo and Friends, his name appears at Fulton's General Store in Port Orleans Riverside, and again at Downtown Disney, in the lessee-operated restaurant Fulton's Crab House.

50

A wall-sized screen in one corner of the Seas with Nemo and Friends was the former home of Turtle Talk with Crush.

When it originally opened, Turtle Talk with Crush was found in the bay nearest the manatee exhibit, but the lack of a dedicated waiting area made for long lines in the central courtyard of the pavilion. Turtle Talk moved in 2007, three years after its initial opening, to the current location near the ride. When it departed, the main screen once used to display Crush remained, and now provides only atmosphere, as though the aquarium extends to this side of the pavilion.

FURTHERMORE: The illusion of the Seabase being on the ocean floor is a carefully cultivated one that dates back to this pavilion's roots as the Living Seas. As Seabase Alpha on the bottom of the ocean, this pavilion was supposedly deep underwater, and large half-domes in the ceiling of the main area attested to this fact. Inside, projected lights created the illusion of sunlight rippling across the surface of the ocean, ostensibly far above us. This effect dates back to the original Seabase Alpha. Those domes in the ceiling still exist, though the special effect has been turned off. A similar effect of water rippling can still be seen in the second floor, just above the waiting area for Turtle Talk.

51

A plaque outside the Land pavilion refers to symbiosis, the original guiding principle behind the pavilion.

All attractions in the original pavilion made reference to the need for a balanced approach to humanity's interaction with nature: they were the Kitchen Kabaret animatronic stage show (balanced nutrition), the Listen to the Land boat ride (balanced approach to farming), and the film actually named *Symbiosis* (balanced relationship with the land).

FURTHERMORE: Elements of this philosophy can still be glimpsed in the décor of the Land pavilion, where colorful balloons in the central courtyard, as well as the name of the nearby food court, make reference in their markings to the four seasons, as if implying the need for a harmonious relationship with nature through all the seasons. These balloons were originally decorated to symbolize the basic food groups.

52

The Land displays one of the old pavilion symbols.

When EPCOT Center was new, each pavilion of Future
World had its own unique stylized symbol. As the
pavilions were updated in the 1990s and beyond, these
symbols were phased out of active use, and the one at the
Land was officially retired in 2005 when the area was
refurbished and re-themed for the opening of Soarin'.
However, the symbol, a leaf in a globe, remains on the
FASTPASS machines at Living with the Land and
provides a link to the past.

FURTHERMORE: The movie *Circle of Life: An Environmental
Fable* (1995) replaced *Symbiosis*, an eighteen-minute video about
the complex interrelationship between humans and the earth, but
some of the scenes in *Symbiosis* were kept intact for the new movie
and can still be seen today. The pavilion's emphasis on the living
plants of the planet is obvious (despite the presence of so many
plastic plants in the non-greenhouse sections of Living with the
Land), but the pavilion also honors the physical earth and its
multifarious composition via the jumbled tile murals just outside the
main doors, meant to capture the layers of the planet's crust.

53

A subtle sign in Living with the Land honors the year Epcot first opened.

The mailbox at the farmhouse has hand-drawn lettering saying "B. Jones 82," a reference to the park's opening in 1982. Then known as EPCOT Center, it was the first theme park opened by Disney which was not a traditional Magic Kingdom, so its turn toward "edutainment" in such attractions as the Land pavilion was a deliberate strategy to imbue the park with an experimental flavor, the better to distinguish it from its Magic Kingdom cousin.

FURTHERMORE: Actual trees were used as specific models when creating the molds for the artificial trees in the opening scenes of the boat attraction. The large sycamore outside the farmhouse, for instance, is a duplicate of one standing outside a car wash in Burbank, California—home to the Walt Disney Studios.

54

The mechanized buffalo and prairie dogs in Living with the Land were originally created for a ride in the Magic Kingdom.

When the Magic Kingdom first opened, it did not have a long, immersive boat ride with robotic performers. The designers thought there would be no interest in a duplicate of Pirates of the Caribbean from California, since Florida was so close to the real Caribbean. Instead, they designed Western River Expedition, a boat ride through desert buttes and misadventures with all sorts of figures from the Old West. However, visitors asked for Pirates of the Caribbean so often that the Western River Expedition idea was shelved and Pirates of the Caribbean was built instead. The buffalo and prairie dogs, which had already been built, were simply put into storage until they were resurrected at Epcot.

FURTHERMORE: Many of the design elements for Western River Expedition ended up being recycled in Big Thunder Mountain Railroad. The Magic Kingdom's version of the ride uses Monument Valley as its stylistic template, which matches the plans for Western River Expedition. In fact, the runaway mine train concept itself started as Thunder Mesa, a mountainous portion of the planned Western River Expedition.

55

One awkward cut in the preshow video at Soarin' reveals its West coast origins.

Many folks may realize that Soarin' was a transplant from Anaheim's Disney's California Adventure, where it was called Soarin' Over California. The ride showcases only vistas from the Golden State and ends with Disneyland, and the preshow video lists only cities in California. But the host on the video, played by Patrick Warburton, actually mentions the name of the ride: "Hello, and welcome to Soarin'." Visitors paying close attention will realize the actor's mouth shuts unnaturally quickly, for this is the result of editing the video and audio away from the original line: "Hello, and welcome to Soarin' Over California."

FURTHERMORE: Soarin' Over California was famously greenlit because the designer had crafted a scale model out of off-the-shelf toy erector sets that demonstrated his idea for a retractable hang-gliding simulator. The attraction features not only, but two Hidden Mickeys: the more obvious mouse symbol made out of fireworks recalls the effect seen in Disneyland's then-current nightly fireworks, Believe, and the less-obvious Mickey can only be seen by those with quick eyes, on the golf ball hit toward the screen. The golfer? None other than then-CEO of the Walt Disney Company, Michael Eisner.

56

A contraption near the ceiling in MouseGear was a prop used in the original Imagination pavilion.

Dreamfinder, who hosted the show with Figment's assistance, was seen in the original attraction flying through the sky in the "Dream Vehicle," an elongated bulbous vehicle held aloft by an overhead balloon as it traveled through the skies gathering dreams. The large metallic vehicle used in the attraction is now on display atop a shelf near the ceiling, opposite the cash registers in MouseGear.

FURTHERMORE: There have been several incarnations of the Imagination attraction. The original Journey Into Imagination was an Omnimover-type ride, with vehicles first circling a round stage that contained the flying Dream Vehicle before entering the larger, more traditional journey through sets that imaginatively explored numbers, letters, painting, and science.

57

The theme song for the original Imagination pavilion is honored in today's attraction.

In the climactic scene of the ride, multiple Figment figures are performing various creative activities. Near the center of the set hangs an oversized poster of sheet music for the song "One Little Spark," the theme song of the original version of the ride. An interim update of the attraction that introduced the Imagination Institute without Figment and the Dreamfinder did not play the song, but the modern version of the ride did bring back the melody as an underscore and theme during key moments of the show.

FURTHERMORE: The same sheet of music in the finale offers a second nod to the past in the form of a silhouette of the Dream Vehicle—that bulbous contraption that flew through the sky with the aid of a balloon—at the very top of the sheet of music. Sharp-eyed visitors can spot another reference to the Dreamfinder: the cartoon of Figment seen in his upside-down house includes a segment where Figment dresses up in Dreamfinder's distinctive magician-like red hat and cape.

58

A doorway halfway through Journey Into Imagination with Figment offers tribute to his onetime co-host of the attraction.

The sets of the current ride were created for Journey into Your Imagination, a Figment-free attraction that was embellished by adding Figment back into it. But Figment got his start in the original Journey into Imagination ride, where he and the Dreamfinder took visitors through bizarre sets to illustrate the variability of imagination and creativity. The Dreamfinder is now referenced just after the Smell Lab, on a door that is labeled "Dean Finder."

FURTHERMORE: Even in the version of the ride that did not include Figment and the Dreamfinder, a tribute was left in the form of a "Hidden Figment" in the queue. When viewed from the right angle, sculpted blue pieces of putty on the middle shelf in a wire storage cage form Figment's shape. This tribute remained even after Figment returned to the ride.

59

The last set in Journey Into Imagination with Figment makes reference to the former Horizons pavilion.

The video of Dr. Nigel Channing (Eric Idle) as the face of the moon recalls a key moment in Horizons, when the Jules Verne story "From the Earth to the Moon" was showcased as one of the visions of the future. In that scene, an animatronic man is catapulted to the moon in a large bullet, and a snippet of George Melies's 1902 adaptation called *A Trip to the Moon* was also visible nearby, in which the moon's entire surface is covered by a face…and the spaceship-bullet lodges itself in one of its eyes.

FURTHERMORE: The attraction incorporates other tributes as well. An ostensible computer control room for the Imagination Institute pays reference to yet another "mad scientist" movie in Disney's film vault, the 1969 movie *The Computer Wore Tennis Shoes*, featuring Kurt Russell. To honor the movie, the room-sized computer in the Imagination pavilion actually has a pair of shoes at its base, and a letterman jacket from Medford (the college at which the action in the movie takes place) hangs on a nearby peg.

60

Gran Fiesta Tour honors a former ride in the Magic Kingdom.

Several of the interior scenes of the attraction inside the Mexico pavilion, Gran Fiesta Tour, are homages to similar moments from a dark ride in the Magic Kingdom called "If You Had Wings." Examples include the lakeside temple scenes, cliff divers and beachgoers, and street peddlers desperate to unload their goods. Even the same songwriter, X Atencio, had written the theme songs for both attractions. An instrumental version of the theme song from "If You Had Wings" can still be heard at Cosmic Ray's Starlight Café.

FURTHERMORE: Until its 2007 refurbishment, the Gran Fiesta Tour was known as El Rio Del Tiempo, when it offered a more relaxing journey through Mexico, by explicitly pointing out the country's history. For that reason, the initial tunnel was framed by paintings of conquistadors. These paintings remain in the modern attraction, although the ride is no longer presented as a historically-informed tour, but rather a search for Donald Duck, so that he can perform at a concert that same evening.

61

The molds for many of the Viking figures in Maelstrom came from other Epcot attractions.

Although external sculpting was done fresh for the figures, the basic molds for the figures in the Norway pavilion attraction were taken from figures done for Spaceship Earth and World of Motion to save costs, and because those rides had many dozens of pre-made molds from which to choose.

FURTHERMORE: A talking bench next to the theater at the conclusion to the ride marks only one of the many interactive creations at Disney World. Countless items in Mickey's and Minnie's walkthrough houses in Mickey's Toontown Fair respond when touched or prodded. Even more responsive is a live-interaction talking trashcan frequently seen in the Magic Kingdom's Tomorrowland. Because a live operator is controlling it remotely, it can respond personally and to changing stimuli. A similar remote controlled 'robot' at Disney's Animal Kingdom takes the form of a "living palm tree."

62

Remnants of a once-planned Africa pavilion remain between the China and Germany pavilions.

The minimal theming done here was simultaneously a test of color and thematic matching with its surroundings and an attempt to entice some African governments to sponsor a pavilion at Epcot. When sponsorship never materialized, the area became a minor shopping and refreshment area.

FURTHERMORE: Other planned exhibits include one dedicated to Russia, with enormous onion domes and a ride, and one for Switzerland, which would have brought a version of Disneyland's Matterhorn roller-coaster to Epcot. A trip down the Rhine river was also planned for the Germany pavilion. In all cases, the lack of sufficient sponsorship spelled the end to the projects.

63

Designers of the American Adventure attraction left behind images of themselves.

The original show director for the American Adventure, Rick Rothschild, can be found in the attraction's lobby as a silhouette portrait just to the right of the entrance door, though a phony ponytail has been added to his profile. The other silhouette portraits are other Imagineers who worked on the project. They had these silhouettes created right at the Magic Kingdom's Main Street store.

FURTHERMORE: Other Imagineer luminaries can be briefly glimpsed in the attraction itself. Legends John Hench, Marty Sklar, and Randy Bright appear in the painting of the victory parade as spectators on the side of the road. As the camera pans out, first Sklar becomes visible above the flutist, then Hench with one hand raised in the air, and finally Bright, with two hands in the air. All three were involved in the creation of this seminal attraction.

64

The "Two Brothers" song in the American Adventure originated at Disneyland's Great Moments With Mr. Lincoln attraction.

During the film that plays during the "Two Brothers" song at the American Adventure, a train depot is shown, which was once Disneyland's Frontierland train station, a set of buildings opposite the tracks in Anaheim that nowadays function only as decoration.

FURTHERMORE: The America pavilion makes use of "forced perspective" in a fashion opposite from the usual. Disney designers frequently employ this moviemaker's trick to make objects appear taller than they really are by shrinking down the overall size of doors, windows, and other features, particularly near the top of a structure. At the America pavilion, an opposite effect is used. Because the building represented a visual focal point as visitors transitioned from Future World to World Showcase, it was built five stories tall—anything less would not be imposing enough from across the lagoon. However, Colonial buildings were not taller than three stories, so this structure had to be tall but look like a naturally-sized three stories. The forced perspective employed resulted in some oversized doors and windows even on the ground floor.

65

The American Adventure, in telling its story chronologically and with an emphasis on realism, only makes use of photographs and film footage after the camera is invented.

To maintain as accurate a presentation as possible, no photographic or filmic reproductions of the events before the invention of the camera are shown in the attraction. Instead, hand-drawn paintings are used to accompany the voiceover narration. Only once the show reached the Civil War, a time when real photographs were available as references, does the show begin to make use of pictures and video.

FURTHERMORE: The focus on realism led designers to purchase actual antique props and pieces of furniture for the parts of the attraction with sets for *Audio-Animatronics* figures. The banjo player's shoes, for instance, were found in an abandoned relief mission in Los Angeles. Additionally, the figures are outfitted with expensive wigs woven from real human hair in an attempt to maximize their natural appearance.

Disney's Hollywood Studios

66

One shop on Sunset Boulevard replicates the theater which originally premiered *Snow White and the Seven Dwarfs.*

The Once Upon a Time store halfway down the street is fashioned to be reminiscent of the Carthay Circle Theater, the location in Hollywood that marked the world premiere in 1937 of *Snow White and the Seven Dwarfs* (it was also the location of the 1929 premiere for the first Silly Symphony, *Skeleton Dance*). A mural inside the Hollywood and Vine restaurant prominently features the Carthay Circle Theater, with *Snow White and the Seven Dwarfs* listed in the mural as the marquee film.

FURTHERMORE: Contractor stamps in the sidewalk of Sunset Boulevard pay respect to Mickey Mouse's original name, Mortimer Mouse. The stamps say "Mortimer & Co. Contractors, 1928"—the same year that Walt Disney lost creative control of Oswald the Lucky Rabbit and invented Mickey Mouse instead. A plaque at the FASTPASS machines for Tower of Terror likewise refers to 1928, in this case as the founding date for Sunset Hills Estates. Other references to 1928 can be seen atop the building at the corner of Hollywood and Sunset and above the restaurant named "Hollywood and Vine." These and many other dates found nearby reinforce the area's theme as Hollywood set in the late 1920s and early 1930s.

67

Letters spilled from the menu board between the libraries at Tower of Terror offer an inside joke.

The old-style menu sign is missing several of its letters, which have fallen to the base of its enclosed box. Visitors who peer into the menu box will see these letters jaggedly spelling out "EVIL TOWER U R DOOMED." This detail is all the more impressive for being so inconspicuous and is probably only seen by visitors who stumble across it by accident.

FURTHERMORE: The Tower of Terror frequently pays such exquisite attention to detail. French bronze statues in the lobby are complimented by authentic antique chairs from the Portuguese Renaissance. There's even a "Hidden Mickey" in the video which explains the attraction in the form of a Mickey Mouse doll held by the little girl authentic to the period, one of the first such dolls ever made in the 1930s. The Mah Jongg game in the lobby was played by championship players; designers were so interested in authenticity that professional players were called in to play a game on this board for sixty minutes. At the end of the hour, they simply stood up and left the board as it can be seen today, lending the appearance of both accuracy and sudden disappearance.

68

The Tower of Terror includes several references to the television show, *The Twilight Zone*, that inspired its theme.

Dozens of references scattered around the attraction pay tribute to various episodes of the famous black and white show. In the library, visitors can see a small red machine that answers yes or no questions and a book called *To Serve Man*. Inside the elevator, an inspection certificate is numbered 10259—a reference to the very first airing of the show on October 2, 1959. After the drop, the basement contains still more references to the show, such as a slot machine and a ventriloquist's dummy.

FURTHERMORE: Some episodes are even given multiple references. There's one well-known episode called "Time Enough at Last," in which Burgess Meredith's character gets the entire world to himself with no interruptions, and he can finally settle down to read all the books he's wanted to over the years…but almost immediately he breaks his glasses and cannot see. This is referenced twice in the ride; once in the library with a pair of broken glasses, and again in a display case in the exit area of the ride containing personal notices, one of which says "lost—reading glasses, horn rim, thick lenses."

69

Ride and show designers left traces of themselves at the Rock 'n' Roller Coaster.

Disney artists and engineers who designed the attraction left behind their initials and birthdays on electrical boxes in the queue area, most notably the dispatch console and a box right at the point where the trains launch. The street address for Walt Disney Imagineering in Glendale (1401 Flower St.) adorns one wall near to that launch point, while the nearby chain-link fences include mention of Buena Vista, which is not only the name of an important Disney subsidiary, but also the street on which the Disney studio first began.

FURTHERMORE: Imagineers have a long history of granting themselves immortality in their rides, such as the initials that adorn several baskets in the Star Tours queue, a practice started in Anaheim's version of the attraction and continued in Orlando. Imagineers' initials can also be seen on pipes and crates at the Living Seas. Over at the Sci-Fi Dine-In Restaurant, the license plates on each of the cars indicate initials and birthdays of the Imagineers.

70

One scene in the movies of the Sci-Fi Drive-In Theater was also once part of Space Mountain.

A humanoid robot named Garco makes a brief appearance in a montage of old film clips in the Sci-Fi Drive-In Theater, but he had once also appeared in "Space Mountain TV," a video in the queue of Space Mountain that showed ostensible channel-surfing through Fed-Ex commercials and whimsical news shows. There identified as Galactic President Garco, he actually traces his lineage on film to a 1957 episode of the show "Disneyland," on an episode called "Mars and Beyond" that postulated life on Mars.

FURTHERMORE: That queue video at Space Mountain was rife with references to old Disney properties. One could glimpse the ship from Flight of the Navigator, visible when Crazy Larry tried to sell used spaceships. And Crazy Larry was himself famous in Disney circles: the actor was Charles Fleischer, voice of Roger Rabbit. There was a Hidden Mickey in the form a satellite unfurling radio antenna ears, as well as a tribute to the old ride Mission to Mars, in the form of a downward view of a rocket launching that was once part of the attraction.

71

Decorative hieroglyphs hidden in the wall of the Great Movie Ride honor Mickey Mouse and Donald Duck.

Mickey, dressed as a Pharaoh, is being served food by Donald, shown as a slave, in a stone carving in the Indiana Jones room of the Great Movie Ride, opposite the scene where the ark of the covenant is being opened. Set slightly above visitors' heads, this block is seldom noticed unless sought directly. It can be seen to the left of the ride vehicle, after passing the second Anubis statue and in the corner of the room, about halfway up the wall.

FURTHERMORE: Part of the decorations elsewhere in the same room is a tribute to R2-D2 and C3PO, the droid partnership from the *Star Wars* movies. They are drawn as symbolic hieroglyphic symbols, rather than more direct representations like Mickey and Donald. The connection with Indiana Jones is a fairly direct one, since George Lucas was the creative force behind both franchises.

72

The swinging Tarzan in the Great Movie Ride was duplicated for Disneyland Paris.

When building the French version of Pirates of the Caribbean, designers wanted to inject additional excitement into the attraction in the form of sets and elements not found in the American versions of the ride. One such innovation was a pirate swinging from a rope right over the boat full of Guests. The Tarzan figure from the Great Movie Ride provided a ready-made mold for the Paris attraction; they merely had to change its costume and duplicate the figure.

FURTHERMORE: The Great Movie Ride is often noted for its use of a Hidden Minnie (not a Hidden Mickey) in the mural at the loading dock. But there is a Hidden Mickey nearby. Before Sunset Blvd and the sorcerer hat were added, the central plaza was laid out to represent a giant Hidden Mickey seen in profile when viewed from the air, with the theater as part of Mickey's mouth and the round Echo Lake as his ear.

73

One billboard near Rock 'n Roller Coaster pays homage to the park's opening date.

The billboard for "Sunset Hills" advertises ostensible homes for sale and lists at the bottom "Hollywood Realty KL5-6189." This is a veiled (and somewhat garbled) reference to May 1, 1989—the first day Disney's Hollywood Studios (then known as the Disney-MGM Studios) was open to the public.

FURTHERMORE: A sign in the Great Movie Ride also uses numbers to allude to history. The scene with an urban shoot-out includes a car full of mechanized gangsters on the right side of our vehicle that has a license plate reading "021-429," a reference to February 14, 1929. This date marked the Valentine's Day Massacre, a bloody execution of rival gangsters thought to have been carried out by Al Capone's men.

74

The plane in the background of the Casablanca set of the Great Movie Ride is not from the movie, yet has its own interesting tale.

Persistent urban legend claims that the plane used in this set comes from the movie *Casablanca*, but there is conclusive evidence that no real plane was used in shooting that scene, and they used a mock-up instead that was smaller in scale. Disney purchased a full-sized, real Lockheed plane for the Great Movie Ride.

FURTHERMORE: The back half of the Disney's Lockheed was put to use elsewhere in the property, at the Magic Kingdom's Jungle Cruise. This prop can be seen near the animatronic of the elephant and the African savannah.

75

Some of the props in the warehouse at the Backlot Tour come from the former attraction World of Motion.

The warehouse used as a queue just before visitors board the trams is crammed full of props used in movies, as well as several artifacts from Epcot's former ride World of Motion, which celebrated the history of transportation. Of particular interest are several robotic performers, now unplugged and stripped of their clothing. Examples include a balloonist, a man strapped to a wooden wing attempting to defeat gravity, and a collection of several masks used to give *Audio-Animatronics* their realistic faces.

FURTHERMORE: While some of the movie props in the warehouse are highly recognizable, such as the rocket backpack from the *Rocketeer* and the taxi cab used in the *Great Muppet Caper*, most of the artifacts appear unremarkable. Yet several are recycled objects from Walt Disney World's history: hitching posts and antique mutoscopes transported from the Magic Kingdom's Main Street welcome visitors to the warehouse, for instance, and banners used in World of Motion adorn one wall.

76

The plane visible on the Backlot Tour is the very one used by Walt Disney to scout the then-undeveloped Walt Disney World property.

"Mickey Mouse One," as the plane was called in reference to the presidential plane Air Force One, is a Grumman G-159 Gulfstream I multi-engine propeller plane built in 1963, used by Walt Disney and later executives as a corporate aircraft, until it was finally decommissioned in the late 1980s and retired to Disney's Hollywood Studios.

FURTHERMORE: While Orlando's main airport saw Mickey Mouse One with regularity, after a while it made sense for Disney to build an airstrip right on Walt Disney World property. Although the idea had been to cater to visitors flying with small commercial airlines from regional airports, Disney's airstrip was never heavily used, as it functioned only as an "uncontrolled" landing strip and could not store many planes. Plans for a Disney-built, wide-winged plane designed for this type of short-takeoff runway (STOLport) never came to fruition, and the airstrip fell into disuse. To this day, the remnants of the airstrip can still be found to the east of the toll booths at the Magic Kingdom's parking lot.

77

References throughout Star Tours and the Indiana Jones Epic Stunt Spectacular honor director George Lucas.

During the overhead announcements in the queue for Star Tours, Lucas' first film, *THX1138*, is mentioned as the license number of a landspeeder "parked in a no-hover zone." The same terminal announcement references George Lucas by saying his name backwards: "Departing Endor passenger, Sacul; Mr. Egroeg Sacul, please see the Star Tours agent at gate number three." One of the crates in the walkway opposite the Indiana Jones Epic Stunt Spectacular is labeled 1138, also in tribute to Lucas's first movie. The nearby counter-service food cart also bears a mention of 1138.

FURTHERMORE: The Star Tours announcements were duplicated from Disneyland, where deliberate homage was paid to "Tom Morrow": "Mr. Morrow, Mr. Tom Morrow, please check with a Star Tours agent at gate number four." Tom Morrow first appeared in Flight to the Moon as the flight control commander, though he was later renamed Mr. Johnson when the attraction was changed in 1975 to Mission to Mars. Since Star Tours appears in Anaheim's Tomorrowland, it seemed an appropriate place to pay tribute to him.

78

A few of the marching soldiers that appear in MuppetVision 3-D can be seen in the ceiling of the preshow area.

Groups of these soldiers, dressed just as they appear in the 3-D movie, can be seen in the rafters above. The preshow is home to numerous inside jokes, such as the spaceship Swine Trek used in "Pigs in Space," a picture of Muppet creator Jim Henson, and even a Hidden Bunsen Honeydew and Beaker (represented as a ball with glasses and a whistle with bulging eyes). Inside the theater itself are further gags, such as the sheet music in front of the penguin orchestra—it's the music for "The Rainbow Connection," a song that appeared in the first *Muppet Movie*.

FURTHERMORE: In typical Muppet style, there are also puns and wordplays scattered about the attraction. The preshow sports a net full of jello (spoken aloud, it sounds like Annette Funicello), as well as a crate labeled 2-D Fruities (i.e., "tutti frutties"). The projector inside the auditorium is labeled as a Yell & Howell model, which is simultaneously a play on words ("yell and howl") and a reference to a prominent manufacturer of projectors named Bell and Howell.

79

A Hidden Kermit in Star Tours pays homage to the tradition of placing Hidden Mickeys on attractions.

Since the studio-themed park wanted to stress Muppets over mice, a non-functioning robot with more than a passing resemblance to Kermit was placed in the second room in the queue where the baskets cycle around overhead, near the first G2 droid we encounter. It reclines as if broken and awaiting repair.

FURTHERMORE: Other characters are hidden in a few locations as well. For instance, there's a Hidden Minnie seen in side profile at the Great Movie Ride; she is located in the loading zone, above a house near the center of the mural.

80

A prop from Adventure Thru Inner Space is visible in the Star Tours film.

Adventure Thru Inner Space, an attraction at Disneyland which had preceded the West Coast version of Star Tours inside one particular building at Disneyland, sported a "Mighty Microscope" in its queue, since that ride pretended to shrink visitors to the atomic level and use microscopes to see them. In the Star Tours movie, this Microscope is visible along the bottom of the screen on the right side, as our Starspeeder zooms out of the hangar. Guests can even see the miniaturized "Atomobiles" (the first usage of the Omnimover system still common at Disney attractions like the Haunted Mansion) in the top of the Microscope as they zoom by.

FURTHERMORE: The G2 droids working the queue are duplicates of the ones in Disneyland's version of the ride, where they were once animated geese removed from Disneyland's America Sings attraction and repurposed as robots. The webbed feet and wagging tail of the droid that is repairing an R2 droid in the second queue room give testament to its avian ancestry. Other robotic animals from America Sings were used at Disneyland's Splash Mountain, so when Orlando's Splash Mountain was constructed, many of the animals chosen simply mirrored the ones repurposed from the old Disneyland ride, such as the vultures just before the drop or the chickens with spread wings on the riverboat at the finale (the original animatronics were singing gospel songs!)

81

A mold for a vehicle once used at Epcot's Horizons can be seen at Backlot Express.

Atop one corner of the dining area in this restaurant is the mold used to create a hovercraft that was used at one scene in Horizons, the former attraction at Epcot. The original pavilion to occupy the spot now taken by Mission: Space, Horizons celebrated the "future that never was," the often quirky visions of the future which never came to pass. The hovercraft still visible today was located in the foreground of a scene where the fruit from orange trees was being harvested by remote-controlled vehicles.

FURTHERMORE: A robotic butler sporting many arms was another iconic scene from Horizons that manages to resurface as part of a video every so often. Disneyland's Innoventions flashes an image of the robotic butler, for instance, as does the "One Man's Dream" movie that Disneyland opened in its Opera House to celebrate its Golden Anniversary in 2005.

82

The dinosaur standing in the lake in Disney's Hollywood Studios honors the early history of animation.

The world's first animated film debuted in 1914, when Windsor McCay released *Gertie the Dinosaur*, a short film in black and white about a sauropod who displays emotions as she interacts with a lake, a sea monster, and a mammoth. In fact, the film was presented as part of a live vaudeville act; McCay would issue Gertie instructions that she would appear to act upon; at one moment, he tosses an apple to her and then one appears on screen. Before Gertie and this act, McCay had faced an uphill battle with his audiences, who were inclined to believe that drawings could not come to life. Walt's Laugh-O-Grams and Alice Comedies of the 1920s owed much to McCay's innovations, and when Walt later met McCay's son, he stressed how much he owed McCay for his trailblazing.

FURTHERMORE: Crates across the lake near the Dockside Diner offer references to famous movies. There's one crate addressed to Rick's Café Americain in Casablanca, another to Scarlett O'Hara, one from the Rosebud Sled Company, one earmarked for Max Bialystock, a primary character in *The Producers*, and a final one for George Bailey, the main character from *It's a Wonderful Life*.

Disney's Animal Kingdom

83

Docks on either side of Discovery Island were once used for boats that transported guests around the park's waterways.

Originally known as the Discovery River Boat Tour, this attraction suffered long lines and little to look at, so by the end of 1998 it was renamed the Discovery River Taxis, to point out that its function was transportation. That too did not grab the public's attention, and for most of 1999 it was known as the Radio Disney River Cruise, aimed at younger audiences, until it finally closed for good in August 1999.

FURTHERMORE: The five boats in the fleet (Crocodile Belle, Darting Dragonfly, Hasty Hippo, Leaping Lizard, and Otter Nonsense) cruised past a few points of interest, like frothy bubbles near Africa meant to imply an underwater creature, or a full-size animated Iguanadon standing in shallow water near Dinoland. The boats can sometimes be seen today transporting a live band playing amplified music in the Asia/Dinoland lagoon.

84

Buildings at Disney's Animal Kingdom are intentionally kept shorter than the surrounding landscape.

The chief designer at Disney's Animal Kingdom, Joe Rohde, decreed that no buildings taller than 30 feet could be built without his explicit permission, to keep nature supreme in the park. For this reason, plants are not trimmed and landscape is meant to be dominant, rather than architecture. The two biggest features of Disney's Animal Kingdom skyline, a tree and a mountain, also adhere to this principle.

FURTHERMORE: For this reason, the first section of Disney's Animal Kingdom does not consist of rows of buildings, as can be found at other parks, but giant shoots of bamboo and other tall trees. Natural features, as well as man-made ones camouflaged to look natural, are used in place of fences to keep the animals in the safari in their enclosures.

85

A solitary stone dragon visible from the bridge to Camp Minnie-Mickey honors a onetime idea for a new land.

Beastlie Kingdomme, a land of mythical creatures that never lived, was meant to be built near here in the area now occupied by Camp Minnie-Mickey, but the idea lost out to the need for more children's areas in the park. Land was set aside on the other side of Camp Minnie-Mickey, which was conceived with an Adirondack theme to blend more naturally into the fantasy realm, should that ever be built after all.

FURTHERMORE: When the Discovery River Boat Tour was transporting visitors around the park's waterways, the stone dragon was one of the primary show elements, spewing flames each time a boat came close.

86

Dragon designs on benches throughout the park make reference to Beastlie Kingdomme.

Dragons were part of the original plan for expansion of this park right from the beginning. To this day, the official logo for Disney's Animal Kingdom features a dragon silhouette as part of the Tree of Life; this logo can be seen throughout the park on trash cans and other locations.

FURTHERMORE: Even the ticket booths in front of the park made reference to the original plan to build the park's thematic foundation on the triumvirate of real animals, prehistoric ones, and imaginary ones. A carved representation of an elephant's head adorns the roof of one ticket booth, with a second booth hosting a triceratops, and the third home to a dragon's head.

87

The minimally-animated, oversized puppets in the Festival of the Lion King come from Disneyland.

A former daytime street parade named the Lion King Celebration at Disneyland featured the giraffe, elephant, Simba, and Pumbaa that now form the centerpieces of the large float units for the show in Disney's Animal Kingdom.

FURTHERMORE: There is a long tradition of re-using parade elements in a more permanent fashion whenever possible. For instance, the golden camels that today spit water at the Magic Carpets of Aladdin come from a parade at Disney's Hollywood Studios called Aladdin's Royal Caravan, though they had been temporarily relocated to the Soundstage restaurant after the parade's end.

88

The Tree of Life's primary feature of animal carvings is an idea borrowed from Bali.

The concept of carving animal figures into the branches and trunk of a tree, such as taken to extremes on the Tree of Life, is a practice taken from Bali. Meanwhile, the architecture on Kali River Rapids is inspired by sources in Thailand, Java, and Nepal.

FURTHERMORE: The Tree of Life is a massive structure that called for a unique metal framework. Because it needed to house a theater inside it and support a 140-foot tall concrete tree above it, the skeleton had to have a distinctive shape. Fortunately, designers didn't have to engineer a framework from scratch: they found just what they needed by modifying an oil rig, such as are frequently used for offshore drilling. The rig conformed to the needed shape but offered enough strength to support the hundreds of branches and thousands of leaves festooned to the exterior alongside the sculpted concrete animal figures.

89

A prominent sculpture of a chimpanzee on the Tree of Life owes its existence to biologist Jane Goodall's visit to the park.

During construction of Disney's Animal Kingdom, famous researcher Jane Goodall viewed the Tree of Life and wondered why there was no chimp prominently represented. Given a chance to remedy that, she chose David Graybeard, a chimpanzee she had known for a long time, to immortalize near the entrance to *It's Tough to be a Bug*, and a plaque was placed nearby to explain Graybeard's significance.

FURTHERMORE: More than 325 animals now grace the Tree of Life, which is an impressive structure all on its own. Made up of three levels of branches (45 main branches, 756 medium branches, and 8,000 smaller branches), these artificial arms support 102,583 leaves—each one more than a foot long. Like the steel skeleton of the tree trunk, the leaves were crafted and attached to withstand winds of nearly 100 mph.

90

Africa is represented by the fictional village of Harambe.

Based on the real town of Lamu in Kenya, Harambe was designed to show the effects of age and change, as a town that once relied on the ivory trade but now turns to tourism instead (a theme echoed by the nearby safari ride). Harambe is modernizing, leading to vestiges of both the old-world culture and the new technologies scattered about the town.

FURTHERMORE: Not all of the technology that is displayed can be considered modern. For instance, one makeshift insulator in the electricity wires overhead is actually a Coca-Cola bottle in a nod to both the inventiveness of African towns and the longtime sponsorship of Disney parks by the Coca-Cola company.

91

The Kilimanjaro Safari is divided into parcels to instill an eco-message of the need for land.

Animals require real estate, and Joe Rohde wanted to emphasize that if we desire to share the planet with animals, we need to dedicate enough space for them to live on. For this reason, all animals at Disney's Animal Kingdom are displayed only in landscape settings rather than more zoo-like enclosures that lack adequate space.

FURTHERMORE: The ecology-friendly message at Disney's Animal Kingdom is taken seriously enough to form the focus of Kali River Rapids, as well as the prominent mural at Conservation Station, where images of animals are colorful at one end of the mural, but fade into black and white at the other, to imply fading into oblivion. In addition, recycling is incorporated into the park's operations in ways unlike any other theme park. The uniforms for many of the Cast Members, for instance, include a pulpy fabric harvested from trees.

92

Asia is represented by the fictional village of Anandapur.

A Sanskrit word that means "the place of delights," Anandapur was inspired by multiple Asian cultures but does have a single, unified backstory to the land. A onetime reserve for hunting, the area sprouted a village and then turned away from hunting to conservation, in an echo of the theme employed in the African section of the park. We might also perceive some clear references to the dangers of extinction, as seen also in Dinoland. Prayer cloths adorning a tree at the front of Asia imbue the area with a tone of authenticity. The land's thematic inspirations from the jungles of Thailand, Indonesia, Nepal, and India were augmented by the Himalayas with the addition of Expedition Everest in 2006.

FURTHERMORE: One photograph in the FASTPASS queue for Expedition Everest shows former Disney executive Frank Wells near the base camp of Mt. Everest. An avid mountain climber, Wells had wanted to conquer the tallest mountain in all seven continents, which is why he is honored on the Magic Kingdom's Main Street windows with the phrase "Seven Summits Expedition." Wells succeeded on six of the seven continents; his two attempts to make it to the summit of Everest were unsuccessful.

93

Highway signs in Dino-Rama honor the opening date of Disney's Animal Kingdom.

Two signs label the main curving road of the land as Highway 498, which reference the opening date of Disney's Animal Kingdom on April 22, 1998. One sign sits near the Boneyard play area, while the other can be found near the road's dead-end alongside Primeval Whirl. A third reference to highway 498 can be seen off to the side of the large Dinosaur billboard at the very end of the road.

FURTHERMORE: The nearby fake gas pump, once located outside but now found inside the store, provides the key to Dinoland's entire theme. The backstory to the land begins with Chester and Hester, who owned a sleepy gas station when dinosaur bones were discovered in the nearby archeological dig. The success of that dig led scientists to take over a shack and expand it with their trailers; this is better known as Restaurantosaurus. The huge fossil dig also lured a modern museum, which houses the ride Dinosaur. Due in part to all their new neighbors and the traffic they attracted, Chester and Hester found it more profitable to sell dino trinkets to visitors than gas, so they converted their store. As sales soared, they expanded into the nearby "parking lot" and built midway games and carnival rides to entertain the travelers.

94

The giant stegosaurus shoulder bone used to create the sign for the Boneyard is actually an outline of the original shape of Disney's Animal Kingdom.

Before Asia was added, the park had a decidedly elongated shape, with a hump off to one side for Camp Minnie-Mickey. An "N" with an arrow on one side of the calcified marquee orients the viewer toward the north, and the bone's shape suddenly makes sense as the park's original outline.

FURTHERMORE: The Boneyard is site of an archeological dig by several professors and their students: Dr. Bernard Dunn, Dr. Shirley Woo, and Dr. Eugene McGee are joined by students Jenny Weinstein, Mark "Animal" Rios, and Sam Gonzales.

95

Restaurantosaurus is themed as a combined lodge and field office for the archeologists supposedly excavating in the area.

The racks of bone specimens in cages can be seen in the temporary-looking additions to the wooden building, as if an existing structure was first taken over as a base of operations by the professors and their students excavating the nearby dinosaurs, and then expanded when more room was needed. The old part of the building has lodge-like features, right down to the stuffed heads of dinosaurs adorning one wall. In the temporary structures, prints on the wall made from palms dipped in black paint form makeshift paintings of various dinosaurs, and testify to the whimsical undercurrent present throughout this land.

FURTHERMORE: The prevalence of whimsy is visible in ways both obvious and hidden throughout the land. The carnival, with its theme of dinosaurs on the brink of extinction and apparently having a party about it, exhibits its whimsy with gusto. But smaller details offer a hint of the same sensibility, such as the set of fossils in the Boneyard play area that emit musical tones when struck: it's a "xylobone."

96

Markings on the walls and vehicles in Dinosaur pay tribute to the attraction's first name.

Originally known as Countdown to Extinction (and abbreviated CTX), the attraction was largely the same experience with a slightly different theme. Parts of the walls and vehicles are still marked "CTX" in reference to the original name of the ride, and numerous references to extinction along the walls of the queue and shop at the exit also pay testament to the ride's original name.

FURTHERMORE: A map of the land located opposite Dino Dig still refers to the attraction building as Countdown to Extinction, not Dinosaur. It reads: "You must go here! It is seriously great!! At COUNTDOWN TO EXTINCTION, they actually send you BACK IN TIME to see LIVE DINOSAURS!! For real!!!"

97

Pipes located in the ceiling at Dinosaur pay tribute to the sponsor of the entire land.

Pipes located overhead in several locations in the loading zone are labeled with the chemical formulas for ketchup, mustard, and mayonnaise, with even the pipes colored red, yellow, and white to further the gag. The reference to condiments honors McDonald's sponsorship of the entire Dinoland USA region of the park.

FURTHERMORE: References to the food chain are common throughout the land. There are food and drink containers with McDonald's logos left, as if discarded, in places like the Boneyard's upstairs archeology office and the back seat of the "road trip" car near Dino-Rama. There are also McDonald's references alongside the model train in the ceiling of Chester's and Hester's Dinosaur Treasures.

98

The time travel corridors in Dinosaur are scaled-up versions of heating coils from toasters.

Disney designers always make a scale model of an attraction before building it; the innards of toasters were used in making the scale model of the two time-travel corridors, and the look of the actual ride was simply copied from the model. Strobe lights and sparks that accompany the effect were inspired by cigarette lighters, simply scaled up twenty times.

FURTHERMORE: A similar use of a scale model influenced the design aesthetic of Soarin'. The chief designer used an Erector set over Thanksgiving weekend to create a working model of his vision for the ride mechanism. When he showed it to the Imagineering team after the holiday, the model worked so well that the final design reflected the look of an Erector set, right down to the ubiquitous holes in the beams.

99

The preshow in Dinosaur provides a thematic link between Disney's Animal Kingdom and Epcot.

Bill Nye provides the voice in the "antiquated" museum preshow to Dinosaur, where his disembodied voice and a few stodgy automated props explain how an asteroid impact doomed the dinosaurs millions of years ago. The presence of Bill Nye supplies a subtle connection to Epcot, where he is co-host of Ellen's Energy Adventure, a ride that similarly makes use of dinosaurs.

FURTHERMORE: A dedication plaque just outside the entrance to the Dino Institute makes a reference to April 22, 1978—a tribute to April 22, 1998, the day that Disney's Animal Kingdom opened. This portion of the institute is meant to portray an old-fashioned (and now out-dated) museum, and placing its supposed birth in the 1970s adds weight to the fiction.

100

Dinoland USA boasts the world's third-largest collection of a particular kind of prehistoric plant.

In an attempt to create a forest worthy of dinosaurs, designers rounded up all the cycads they could find. Cycads are woody plants with cones but look like ferns, and thus can be considered a kind of hybrid creation in the plant kingdom. However, they are more accurately considered living fossils: they flourished in the Mesozoic and were contemporaries of the dinosaurs, which explains their relevance to the land.

FURTHERMORE: The scale of the horticulture at Disney's Animal Kingdom can be breathtaking: there are three thousand species in the safari ride, and forty thousand trees parkwide. More than two and a half million shrubs adorn the park. The collections lend themselves to superlatives: the park has the largest collection of flowering trees in the United States and the largest collection of African species outside of Africa itself.

Walt Disney World General

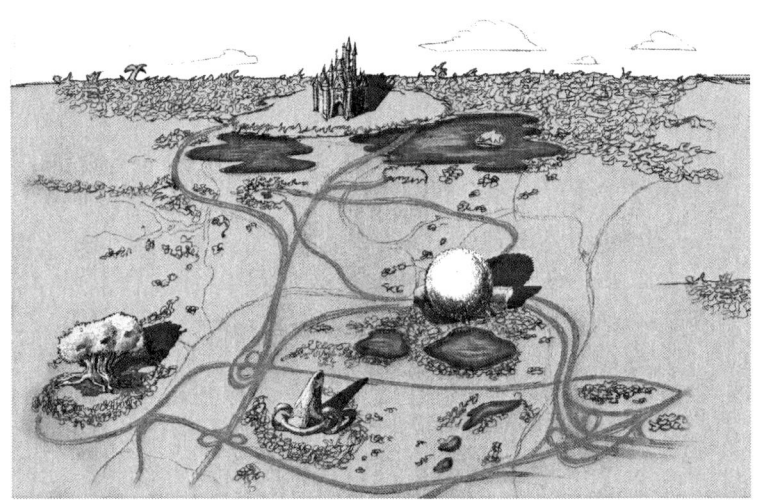

101

Every year about thirty million people visit Walt Disney World, making it one of the top tourist destinations in the United States of America.

While exact numbers are not released, the estimate of thirty million visitors is commonly accepted by industry groups. Not bad for a former swamp then sitting far outside any major city! The Walt Disney Company can realistically be seen as the largest contributing factor to the growth of Orlando and Central Florida. Disney built its theme parks in the middle of nowhere, and still the people descended in droves.

The number of visitors is possibly a better choice than any other tidbit to encapsulate the message of this book: people will come in record numbers to experience the magic Disney produces, and central to the Disney magic are these details and tributes, a combined reverence for the past and for historical accuracy. They create the "Disney Difference" which draws people and keeps them coming back every year for more.

Afterword

While many patrons consciously think only about the rides at Walt Disney World, it's the rich sub-culture of homages, tributes, fun details, intricate trivia, and rich backstories at the parks which do the heavy lifting of enchanting our imaginations.

The Disney attention to detail is legendary, and rightly so. Only by exposing the level to which these details are researched, sought after, refined, and finally implemented can we begin to understand the richness of the tapestry at a Disney theme park. The persuasive tricking of our senses, the completely believable immersion into fictitious realms, and the unconditional suspension of disbelief all owe their existence to such details that seem, at first glance, to be mere adornments, or perhaps even indulgences by the artists.

Don't be fooled. It's the details at Disney that render the experience magical. To know the details is to examine the magician's trick hat—you will have a fuller understanding of what's going on and what to watch for, and it will only increase your enjoyment of the effect.

Kevin Yee

About the Author

Kevin Yee, a Disney fan from birth, spent a decade working at Disneyland and cultivating a never-ending fascination with that park's rich traditions and history. Now relocated to Orlando, Kevin enjoys the Disney offerings on both sides of the country.

Kevin is the author of *The Unofficial Dining Guide to Walt Disney World* (Ultimate Orlando Press), as well as the co-author of two books about Disneyland, *Magic Quizdom* and *101 Things You Never Knew About Disneyland*. These works can be ordered from online bookstores such as Amazon, or from many bricks-and-mortar bookstores directly.

An online journalist and columnist since 1997, Kevin now publishes at MiceAge.com and OrlandoVacation.com.